THE JEWISH
HOLIDAY CRAFT BOOK

This book could only be for Jeannie, who has always done a great job of being the "big sister."
—K.R.

To the loving memory of my parents and the holidays we celebrated together.   —M.L.

Library of Congress Cataloging-in-Publication Data
Ross, Kathy (Katharine Reynolds), 1948-
The Jewish holiday craft book / by Kathy Ross :
illustrated by Melinda Levine.
p. cm.
ISBN 0-7613-0055-4 (lib. bdg.) ISBN 0-7613-0175-5 (trade)
1. Jewish crafts—Juvenile literature. 2. Fasts and feasts—
Judaism—Juvenile literature. I. Levine, Melinda, ill.
II. Title.
BM729.H35R67 1997
296.4´3—dc20 96-31002 CIP AC

Todah Rabah to Rabbi Jon Haddon of
Temple Shearith Israel in Ridgefield,
Connecticut for his many consultations.

Published by The Millbrook Press, Inc.
2 Old New Milford Road
Brookfield, Connecticut 06804

THE JEWISH HOLIDAY CRAFT BOOK

BY KATHY ROSS

ILLUSTRATED BY MELINDA LEVINE

The Millbrook Press
Brookfield, Connecticut

CONTENTS

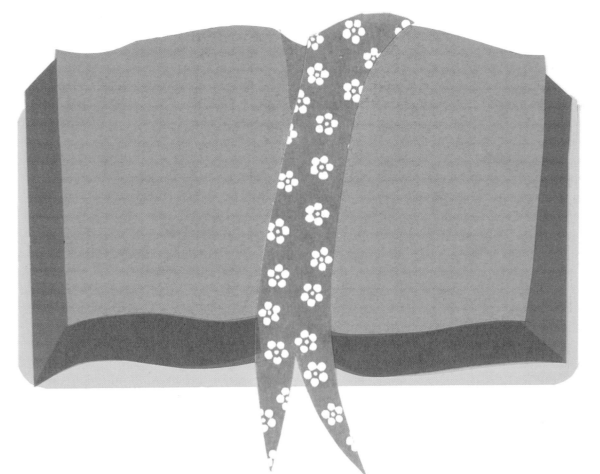

SHABBAT

The Jewish Sabbath, known as Shabbat, begins Friday evening at sundown. The family gathers to light the Sabbath candles. Blessings over a cup of wine and over the challah, a traditional braided bread, begin the joyous Sabbath dinner.

The Sabbath is a day of rest on which people set aside the tasks of the other six days. They visit friends, or read, or do other quiet but pleasurable activities.

Many Jewish families attend Sabbath services at their local synagogue, either on Friday evening or on Saturday morning.

Shabbat ends at sundown on Saturday evening with the celebration of the Havdalah service.

*The Shabbat celebration begins Friday evening
with the lighting of two candles.*

FOIL CANDLEHOLDERS

HERE IS WHAT YOU NEED:

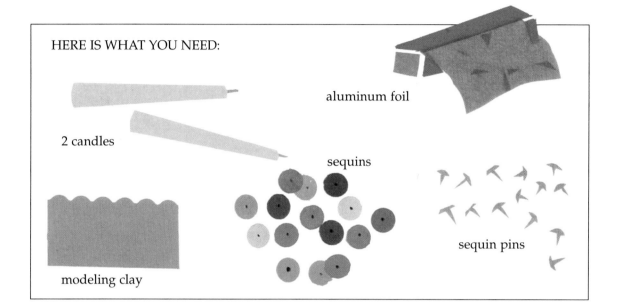

2 candles

aluminum foil

sequins

sequin pins

modeling clay

HERE IS WHAT YOU DO:

1 Roll two identical balls of clay about
2 ½ inches (6.3 centimeters) wide.
Flatten the bottom of each ball by pressing
it lightly on a flat surface. Use the bottom
of one of the candles to create the hole
that will hold the candle in the top of
each ball.

2 Wrap each clay candleholder in aluminum foil, pressing the foil into the hole.

3 Decorate the candleholders by pinning sequins on the foil-covered clay. The pins will slip easily into the clay.

You can also decorate these candleholders using straight pins with colored heads.

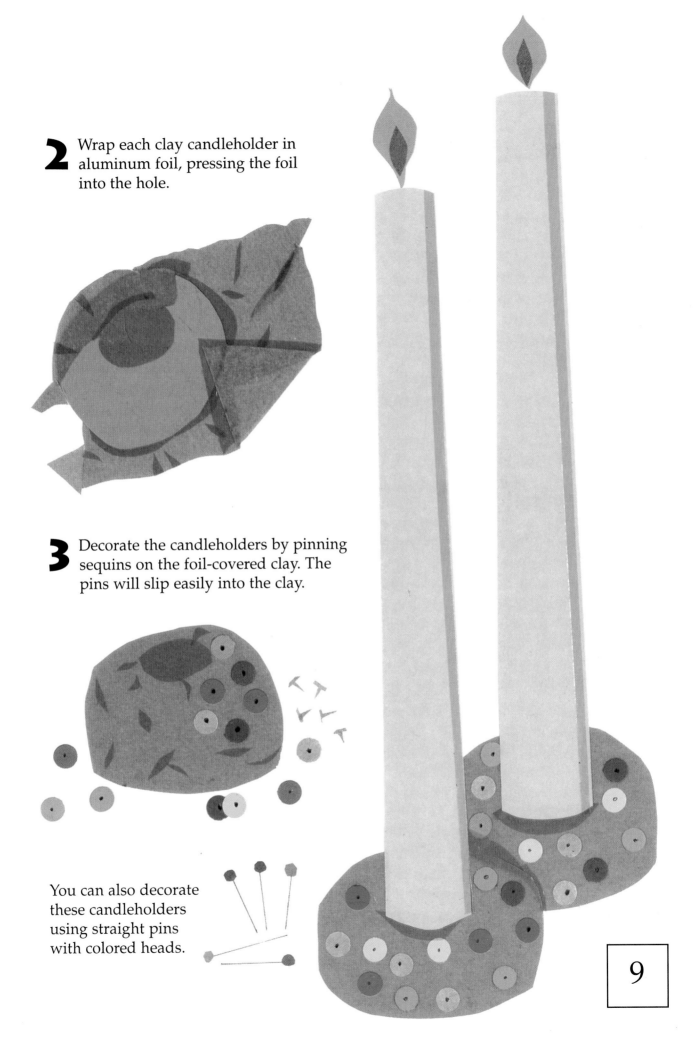

9

Flowers are often used to decorate the Shabbat table.
Surprise your mom by making her this beautiful vase.

NAPKIN-COVERED VASE

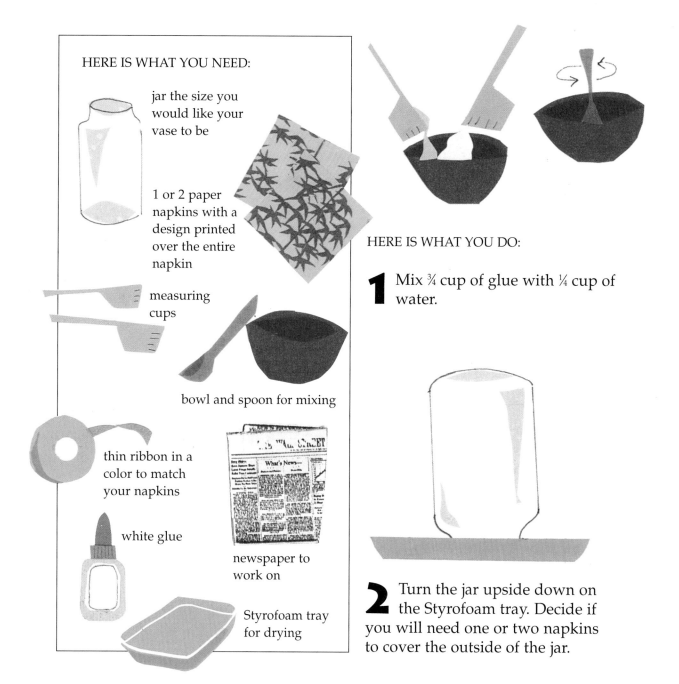

HERE IS WHAT YOU NEED:

jar the size you would like your vase to be

1 or 2 paper napkins with a design printed over the entire napkin

measuring cups

bowl and spoon for mixing

thin ribbon in a color to match your napkins

white glue

newspaper to work on

Styrofoam tray for drying

HERE IS WHAT YOU DO:

1 Mix ¾ cup of glue with ¼ cup of water.

2 Turn the jar upside down on the Styrofoam tray. Decide if you will need one or two napkins to cover the outside of the jar.

3 Carefully dip an unfolded napkin in the water-and-glue mixture. Let the excess liquid drip off, then wrap the napkin around the bottom and outside of the jar. Turn the jar right side up and tuck the edges of the napkin inside the rim of the jar. You may need to overlap a second napkin or part of a second napkin with the first to completely cover the jar.

4 Let the jar dry completely on the Styrofoam tray.

5 Tie a pretty ribbon around the neck of the jar.

11

Kiddush is the blessing over the wine. This Kiddush cup will make a lovely addition to your family's Shabbat celebration.

KIDDUSH CUP

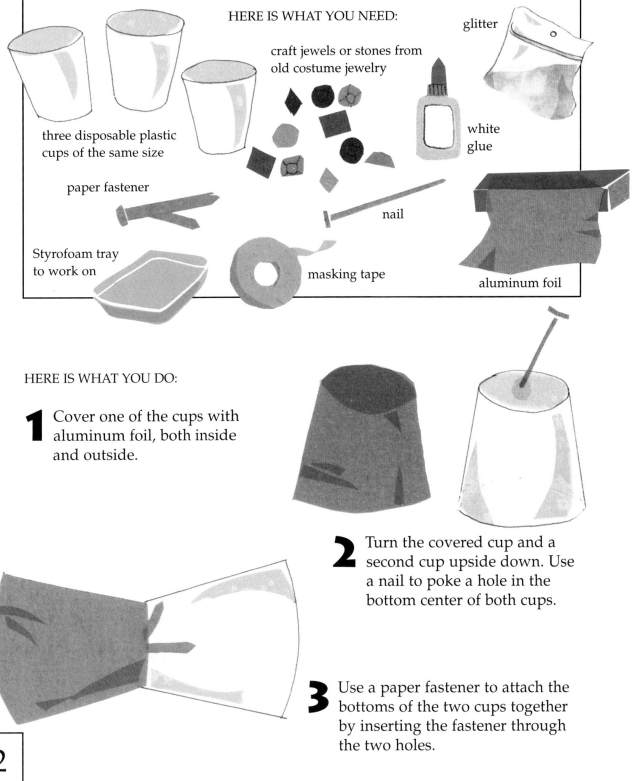

HERE IS WHAT YOU NEED:

glitter

craft jewels or stones from old costume jewelry

three disposable plastic cups of the same size

white glue

paper fastener

nail

Styrofoam tray to work on

masking tape

aluminum foil

HERE IS WHAT YOU DO:

1 Cover one of the cups with aluminum foil, both inside and outside.

2 Turn the covered cup and a second cup upside down. Use a nail to poke a hole in the bottom center of both cups.

3 Use a paper fastener to attach the bottoms of the two cups together by inserting the fastener through the two holes.

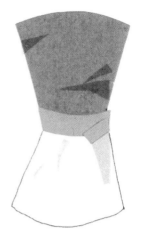

4 Wrap a piece of masking tape around the place where the two bottoms meet.

5 Put tiny pieces of masking tape on the back of each jewel to create a surface that will stick to the cup. Cover the tape wrapped around the cup with glue. Stick jewels all around the tape and then sprinkle glitter around the jewels.

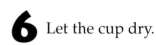

6 Let the cup dry.

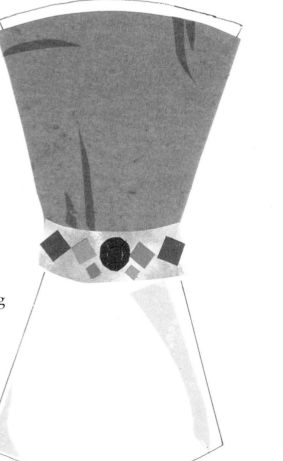

7 Put the third cup inside the foil-lined cup to use as a liner. Your cup can now be used to drink from. The liner may be removed for washing or may be replaced as needed.

The braided loaf of bread served at the Sabbath meal is called challah. It is customary to cover the challah until the blessing is offered.

CHALLAH COVER

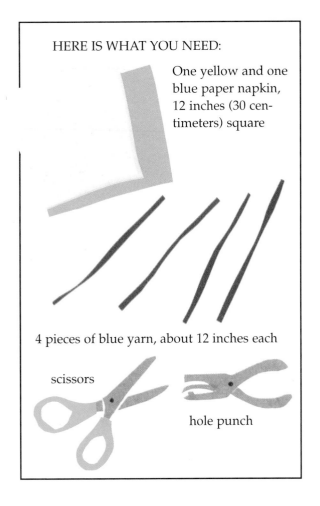

HERE IS WHAT YOU NEED:

One yellow and one blue paper napkin, 12 inches (30 centimeters) square

4 pieces of blue yarn, about 12 inches each

scissors

hole punch

HERE IS WHAT YOU DO:

1 Start with a blue paper napkin folded into a square. Fold the two folded sides of the square over each other the way you would fold a paper to cut a snowflake. Cut small shapes and designs from the folded edges of the napkin. Open the napkin to see the pretty design you have cut.

2 Place the cut blue napkin over the opened yellow napkin. The yellow color will show through the cuts in the blue napkin.

14

3 Use the hole punch to make a hole through both napkins at all four corners, or in the center of each of the four sides. Tie the two napkins together by stringing a piece of yarn through each of the four holes. Tie each piece of yarn in a bow.

Another way to cut the blue napkin is to stencil or draw a simple shape in the center of the folded square napkin. Carefully cut out the shape through the four layers. When you unfold the napkin, you will have the design cut from all four sides of the napkin. You might want to cut the same design from the center of the open napkin also.

Before Shabbat begins, you might want to drop some coins in a tzedakah box. The money from the tzedakah box is to give away to help other people. This tzedakah box can be used year-round by attaching different decorations for different seasons of the Jewish year.

SEASONAL TZEDAKAH BOX

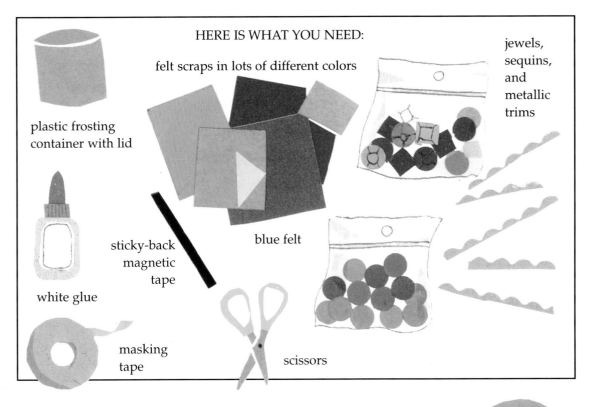

HERE IS WHAT YOU NEED:

felt scraps in lots of different colors

jewels, sequins, and metallic trims

plastic frosting container with lid

blue felt

sticky-back magnetic tape

white glue

masking tape

scissors

HERE IS WHAT YOU DO:

1 Cut a coin slit in the plastic lid of the frosting container.

2 Cover the lid and sides of the container with masking tape to create a surface the glue will stick to. Glue the blue felt onto the masking tape that covers the lid and the sides of the container. Don't forget to cut a slit in the felt over the coin slot in the lid. Do it from the bottom of the lid so you can see where the slit is.

3 Cut a strip of the magnetic tape 1 inch (2.5 centimeters) long and stick it to the side of the container.

4 Cut small shapes from felt to decorate the side of the tzedakah box. Use trim and jewels or sequins to decorate the shapes. Press a piece of magnetic tape to the back of each shape so that it will stick to the magnetic tape on the container.

Make lots of different shapes for the different holidays. Some shapes you might want to make would be a dreidel, stone tablets, a Star of David, a kiddush cup, and a tree. What other shapes can you think of?

A spice box is passed around during Havdalah, the ceremony marking the end of Shabbat.

SPICE BOX

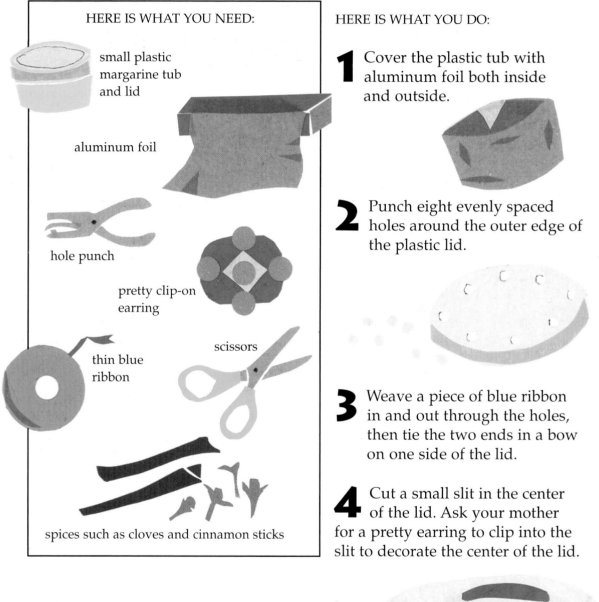

HERE IS WHAT YOU NEED:

small plastic margarine tub and lid

aluminum foil

hole punch

pretty clip-on earring

scissors

thin blue ribbon

spices such as cloves and cinnamon sticks

HERE IS WHAT YOU DO:

1 Cover the plastic tub with aluminum foil both inside and outside.

2 Punch eight evenly spaced holes around the outer edge of the plastic lid.

3 Weave a piece of blue ribbon in and out through the holes, then tie the two ends in a bow on one side of the lid.

4 Cut a small slit in the center of the lid. Ask your mother for a pretty earring to clip into the slit to decorate the center of the lid.

5 Fill your box with spices and place the cover on it.

You will not have to remove the lid to smell the spices. The delicious scent comes right through the holes in the lid.

ROSH HASHANAH

Rosh Hashanah is the beginning of the ten-day period known as the High Holy Days. It is the Jewish New Year. The phrase itself in Hebrew literally means "the head of the year." The holiday is celebrated on the first day of Tishri in the Hebrew calendar. Because the Jewish calendar is lunar, the holiday does not fall on the same day of the secular calendar each year—but it is always in the autumn during the month of September or October.

On Rosh Hashanah people dress in their very best clothes and attend synagogue services. Jews greet each other with the Hebrew phrase "l'shanah tovah tikatevu," which means "may you be inscribed for a good new year in the Book of Life." It is a way of wishing someone Happy New Year.

A traditional food to eat on Rosh Hashanah is apple dipped in honey. Dipping the sweet apple into the even sweeter honey really gets the New Year off to a sweet start!

The shofar is made from a ram's horn. It is blown on Rosh Hashanah and again on Yom Kippur. Make this shofar pin for yourself or someone special to wear during this holiday time.

SHOFAR PIN

HERE IS WHAT YOU NEED:

blue yarn

brown pipe cleaner, 12 inches (30 centimeters) long

scissors

Styrofoam tray for drying

safety pin

white glue

HERE IS WHAT YOU DO:

1 Wrap the pipe cleaner into a horn shape that is small at one end and gets wider and wider.

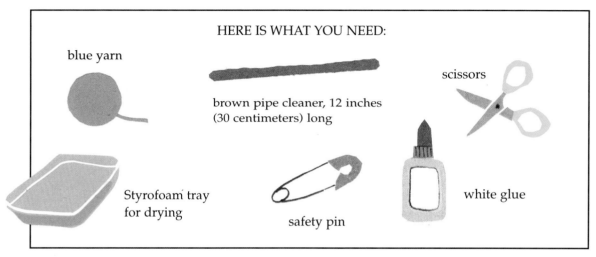

2 Curve your horn shape a bit so that it looks like a shofar. Cover the inside and outside of the shofar with white glue. Let it dry completely on the Styrofoam tray.

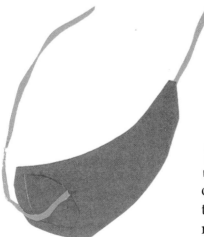

3 Thread a 6-inch (15-centimeter) piece of blue yarn through one end of the shofar and out the other end. Tie the two ends of the yarn together to make a hanger for the pin.

4 Use a safety pin to attach the shofar to a shirt or coat.

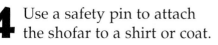

This shofar can be used as a trivet or hung on your door.

TWINE SHOFAR

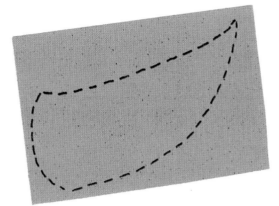

HERE IS WHAT YOU NEED:

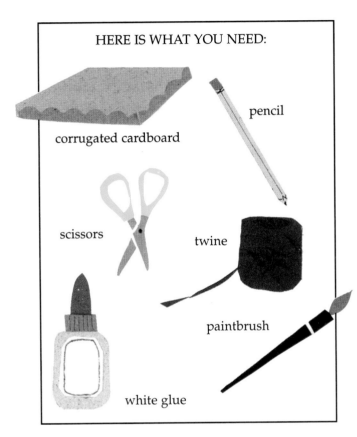

corrugated cardboard

pencil

scissors

twine

paintbrush

white glue

HERE IS WHAT YOU DO:

1 On the corrugated cardboard, sketch a shofar shape that is about 12 to 14 inches (30 to 35 centimeters) long. Cut out the shofar shape.

2 Sketch a round opening at one end of the shofar. Use the paintbrush to cover the opening with glue. Starting at the center of the opening, wrap twine around and around itself until the entire opening is covered.

3 Cover the rest of the shofar with glue, then cover the glue with long pieces of twine. Put a piece of plastic wrap over the shofar and stack some books on it until it dries thoroughly. Then trim the ends of the twine.

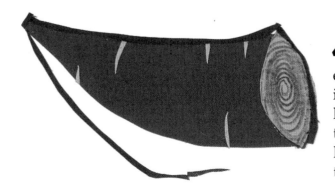

4 Paint glue around the edge of the shofar and wrap the edge with twine to give it a finished look. If you are going to hang the shofar, cut a piece of twine 24 inches (60 centimeters) long and glue the two ends to the back of the horn.

Serve apples and honey in this pretty dish and have a sweet New Year.

APPLE AND HONEY DISH

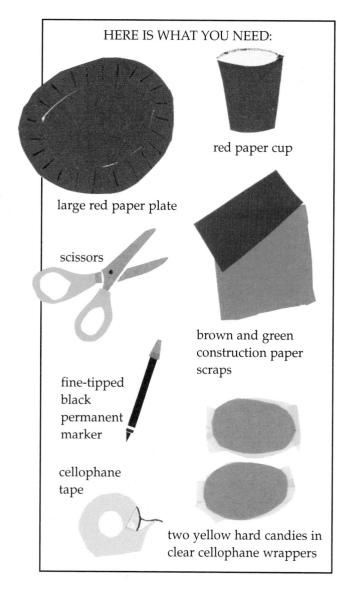

HERE IS WHAT YOU NEED:

large red paper plate

red paper cup

scissors

brown and green construction paper scraps

fine-tipped black permanent marker

cellophane tape

two yellow hard candies in clear cellophane wrappers

HERE IS WHAT YOU DO:

1 Cut an apple stem from the brown paper. Cut an apple leaf from the green paper. Tape the end of the stem and the leaf to the back edge of the red plate so they stick out past the edge of the plate to make it look like an apple.

2 Make eight evenly spaced cuts around the cup that go about two-thirds of the way down the cup. Fold out the cut pieces of the cup to form the petals of a flower. Round off the edges of each petal. Roll a piece of tape so that it is sticky on both sides. Tape the bottom of the flower cup to one side of the apple plate.

 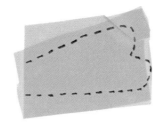 

3 Turn one of the yellow candies into a bee: Use the marker to draw eyes and stripes on the candy wrapper. Open the second piece of candy and cut a pair of wings for the bee from the cellophane wrapper. Tape the wings to the back of the bee. Tape the bee to one of the flower petals.

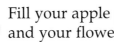

4 Fill your apple plate with apple slices and your flower cup with honey.

*Make these seals to use on envelopes
when you send New Year greetings
to your friends and family.*

NEW YEAR STICKERS

HERE IS WHAT YOU NEED:

measuring cup
and spoons

plain
white
paper

vinegar

permanent
markers

scissors

white
glue

plastic
tub

Styrofoam tray
for drying

HERE IS WHAT YOU DO:

1 Mix about ¼ cup of white
glue with one tablespoon
of vinegar in the plastic tub.
Mix them together well.

2 Draw one or more pictures about
1 to 1 ½ inches (2.5 to 3.8 centimeters)
in height and width that are appropriate for
the season. For example, you might draw a
shofar, a kiddush cup, and a tiny New Year
card. Carefully cut out the pictures.

3 Paint the back of each picture with the glue-and-vinegar mixture. Place each picture face down on the Styrofoam tray to dry.

When you are ready to use your seals, just moisten the backs with water and stick them on an envelope or wherever you wish to use them.

HAPPY
NEW
YEAR

Because it is the start of the New Year, Rosh Hashanah is a time of fresh starts and beginnings.

WHEEL OF MONTHS

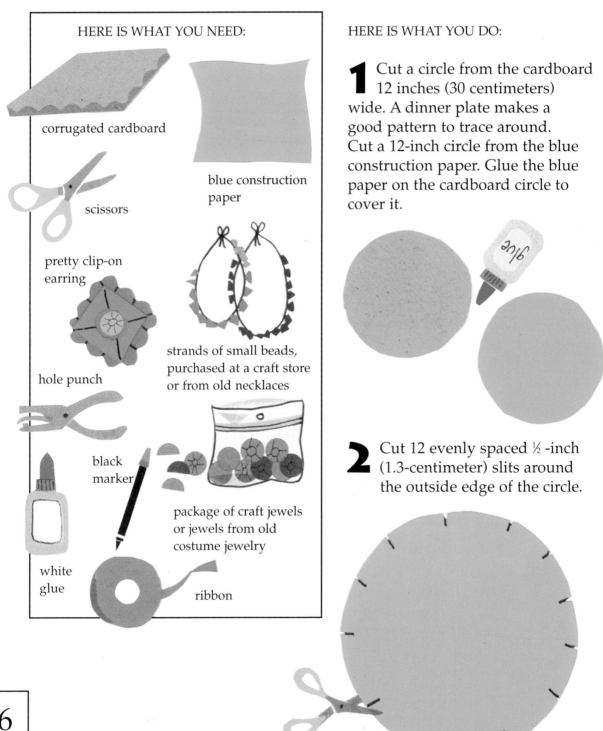

HERE IS WHAT YOU NEED:

corrugated cardboard

scissors

blue construction paper

pretty clip-on earring

hole punch

strands of small beads, purchased at a craft store or from old necklaces

black marker

white glue

package of craft jewels or jewels from old costume jewelry

ribbon

HERE IS WHAT YOU DO:

1 Cut a circle from the cardboard 12 inches (30 centimeters) wide. A dinner plate makes a good pattern to trace around. Cut a 12-inch circle from the blue construction paper. Glue the blue paper on the cardboard circle to cover it.

2 Cut 12 evenly spaced ½ -inch (1.3-centimeter) slits around the outside edge of the circle.

3 Cut six strings of beads, 13 inches (33 centimeters) long. Set each string across the center of the circle with the two ends slipped into the two cut slits across from each other. When you have put the end of a string of beads into each slit, your circle should be divided into twelve equal sections like a pie.

4 Punch a hole in the middle edge of one of the sections. Thread a 6-inch (15-centimeter) piece of ribbon through the hole and tie the two ends together to make a hanger.

5 Starting at the top, write the name of one of the twelve months in each section of the wheel.

6 Glue a jewel on the outer edge of each section.

Use a pretty clip-on earring to mark each month of the year as it comes around.

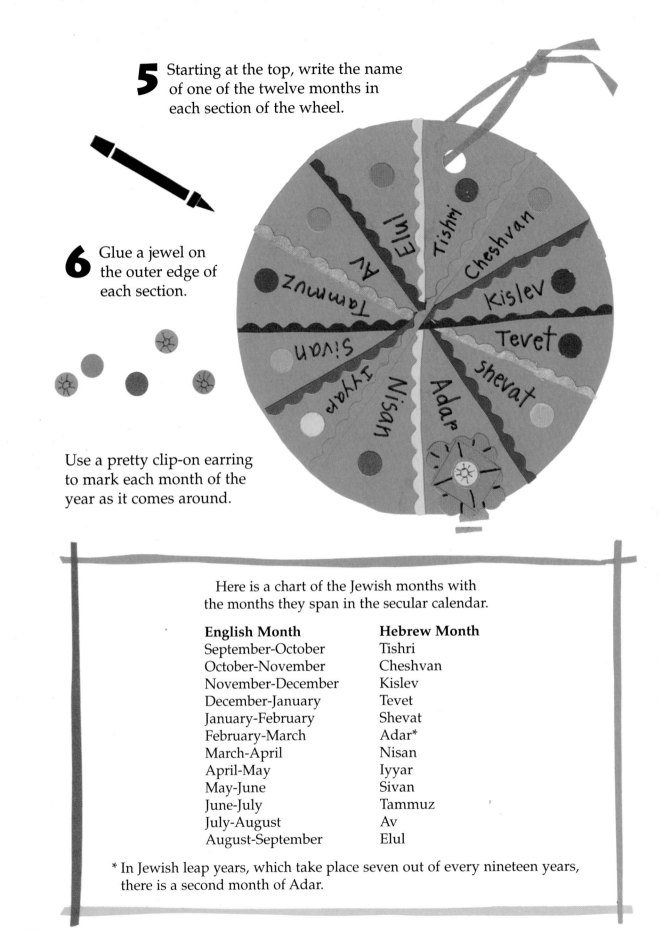

Here is a chart of the Jewish months with the months they span in the secular calendar.

English Month	Hebrew Month
September-October	Tishri
October-November	Cheshvan
November-December	Kislev
December-January	Tevet
January-February	Shevat
February-March	Adar*
March-April	Nisan
April-May	Iyyar
May-June	Sivan
June-July	Tammuz
July-August	Av
August-September	Elul

* In Jewish leap years, which take place seven out of every nineteen years, there is a second month of Adar.

YOM KIPPUR

Yom Kippur is the solemn ending to the High Holy Day period. It falls on the tenth of Tishri in the Hebrew calendar, always ten days after Rosh Hashanah in the secular month of September or October.

Yom Kippur in Hebrew means "Day of Atonement." People ask each other for forgiveness for any harm they may have caused each other, and then offer prayers of repentance to God.

Observant Jews do not eat any food on Yom Kippur. They spend the day in the synagogue praying. When the shofar is sounded for the last time during the High Holy Day period, it means that the Book of Life has now been sealed for the coming year and the observance is over. People gather in homes or synagogues to end the day of fasting with a meal.

The ten days that include Rosh Hashanah and Yom Kippur are a time for thinking about ourselves and how we might better ourselves in the year to come.

OUTSIDE ME AND INSIDE ME DOLL

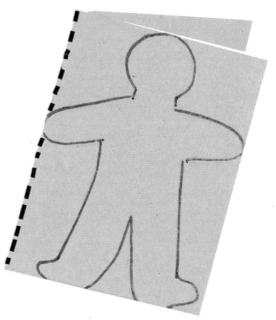

HERE IS WHAT YOU NEED:

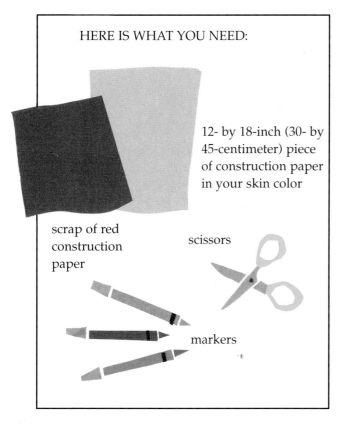

12- by 18-inch (30- by 45-centimeter) piece of construction paper in your skin color

scrap of red construction paper

scissors

markers

HERE IS WHAT YOU DO:

1 Fold the skin-colored construction paper in half. With the fold of the paper at left, so that it opens like a book, draw an outline of a person. Draw the person's left hand right up against the fold of the paper.

2 Use markers to give the person facial features, hair, and clothes to look like you. This is how you look on the outside.

30

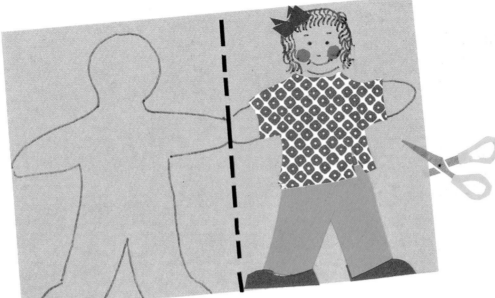

3 Cut the person out of the folded paper leaving the fold at the hand uncut so that the person opens like a card.

4 Cut a heart from red paper small enough to fit inside the paper person. Write something on the heart that you have been thinking about changing. Glue the heart inside the folded person.

The heart tells something about the inside of you. What is in your heart is very important.

When he did not do what God told him to do, Jonah was swallowed by a whale. The story of Jonah is read in the synagogue each year on Yom Kippur.

JONAH AND THE WHALE WATER TOY

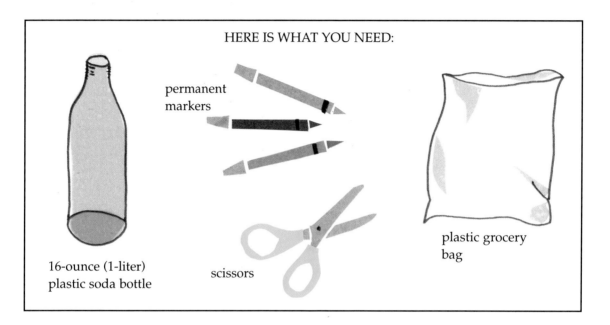

HERE IS WHAT YOU NEED:

permanent markers

plastic grocery bag

16-ounce (1-liter) plastic soda bottle

scissors

HERE IS WHAT YOU DO:

1 Use the permanent markers to add details to the plastic bottle to make it look like a whale. The opening of the bottle should be the mouth of the whale.

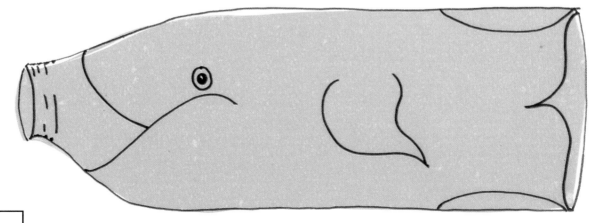

2 Cut a piece of plastic out of the grocery bag, 3 inches (7.5 centimeters) square. Draw a picture of Jonah on the plastic with the markers. Carefully cut out the picture of Jonah.

3 To use your water toy, float Jonah in the water. Give the whale a squeeze and push it down under the water. Swim it over to Jonah and slowly unsqueeze the sides of the bottle. The whale will swallow lots of water and Jonah, too! Give the whale another squeeze and Jonah will pop out again.

This paper whale will swallow Jonah and spit him out again.

JONAH AND THE WHALE PUPPET

HERE IS WHAT YOU NEED:

piece of gray construction paper, 9 by 12 inches (23 by 30 centimeters)

pink and yellow construction paper scraps

black marker

scissors

white glue

brown and red yarn

HERE IS WHAT YOU DO:

1 Fold the gray paper in half lengthwise so that you have a piece of paper that is 4 ½ by 12 inches (11.3 by 30 centimeters). Cut a half heart shape on the fold as large as the paper will allow. This will remain folded and be the body of the whale. Cut a double-pointed fish tail from the gray paper scraps.

2 Glue the whale body together at the top only, so that the front and the back of the whale are open. Glue the tail at the pointed end of the whale body.

3 Use the marker to give the whale an eye and a mouth on both sides.

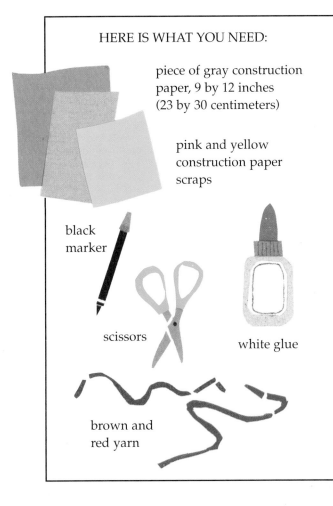

4 To make Jonah, cut a 3-inch (7.5-centimeter) body from the pink paper. Cut a robe for him from the yellow paper and glue it on the body. Draw a face with the marker. Tie a red yarn belt around the waist of the robe. Cut bits of brown yarn and glue them on for the hair and the beard.

5 Cut a piece of brown yarn, 18 inches (45 centimeters) long. Glue the paper Jonah to one end of the yarn leaving about 6 inches (15 centimeters) sticking out above the head. Let the glue dry overnight.

To use the Jonah and whale puppet, string the long end of the yarn through the mouth opening at the end of the whale and out the opening at the tail. To make the whale swallow Jonah, just pull on the yarn at the tail. To make him come out of the whale, pull on the yarn at the mouth of the whale.

The High Holy Days end with our fate for the New Year inscribed in the pages of the Book of Life. What will be written on the pages of your Book of Life this year?

BOOK OF LIFE

HERE IS WHAT YOU NEED:

old, discarded hardcover book

can of gold spray paint

piece of embroidered ribbon, 18 inches (45 centimeters) long

Gold

newspaper to work on

white glue

HERE IS WHAT YOU DO:

1 Ask an adult to help you with the spray painting, best done outdoors. Open the book to about the middle and place it, pages down, on newspaper. Spray the cover and page edges gold. When the paint has dried, turn the book over and spray the inside gold. The paint will cause the edges of the pages to stick together, holding the book in an open position.

2 The ribbon will serve as a bookmark. Glue one end of the ribbon to the top right inside cover of the book. Bring the other end of the ribbon up and over the center of the book to extend about 4 inches (10 centimeters) out from the bottom of the pages.

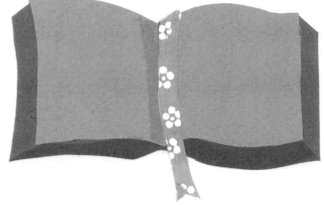

*Make a very special yahrzeit candle
to light on Yom Kippur in memory of
someone important to you who has died.*

YAHRZEIT CANDLEHOLDER

HERE IS WHAT YOU NEED:

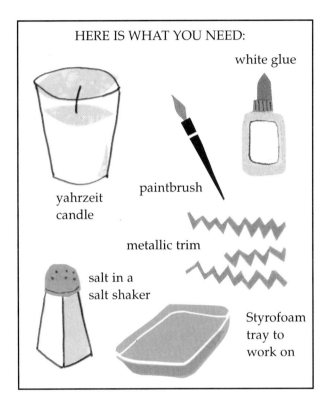

white glue

yahrzeit candle

paintbrush

metallic trim

salt in a salt shaker

Styrofoam tray to work on

HERE IS WHAT YOU DO:

1 Purchase a yahrzeit candle in the Jewish food section of the supermarket or at your synagogue gift shop. It is a heavy glass filled with wax.

2 Paint the outside of the glass jar, except for the rim, with white glue.

3 Hold the jar above the Styrofoam tray and sprinkle the glue-covered jar with salt. The salt and glue will give the jar a glistening surface that looks very pretty with candlelight showing through it.

4 Glue a strip of metallic trim around the rim and the base of the jar.

The blowing of the shofar marks the end of Yom Kippur.

PAPER SHOFAR

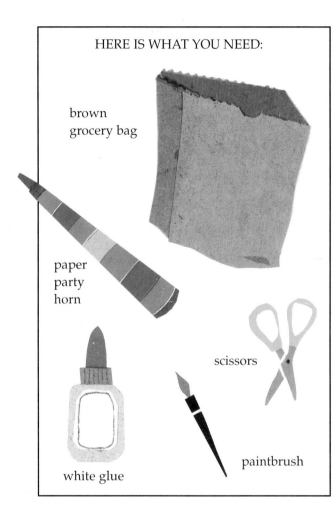

HERE IS WHAT YOU NEED:

brown grocery bag

paper party horn

white glue

scissors

paintbrush

HERE IS WHAT YOU DO:

1 Cut a square piece from the brown bag, 12 inches (30 centimeters) square.

2 Use the paintbrush to spread white glue all over one side of the square.

3 Starting at one corner, roll the square around the party horn and into a cone shape, trimming off any excess.

4 Bend the wide end of the cone shape up about one-third of the way from the end. Let it dry completely to be sure the bent shape will hold.

Now you have your own shofar to blow! It really works!

SUKKOT

Sukkot is the first of the three major festivals of the Jewish year, the other two being Shavuot and Pesach (Passover). Sukkot is an eight-day harvest festival during which Jews express their gratitude for the abundant harvest in many ways.

In the synagogue, the rabbi holds up an etrog, which is a Middle Eastern fruit that looks like a very large lemon. The lulav, a bundle of palm, willow, and myrtle leaves, is shaken in thanks for the greenery that comes forth from the earth.

At home, people build a three-sided outdoor booth known as a sukkah. The roof of the sukkah is covered with greenery and hung with fruits and vegetables. People invite their friends to come and share a meal with them in the sukkah.

Building this sukkah collage will be good practice for building the real thing!

MY SUKKAH

HERE IS WHAT YOU NEED:

photographs of you, your family, and friends

plastic berry basket

6 green pipe cleaners

1 piece of green construction paper

2 pieces of brown construction paper, 12 by 18 inches (30 by 45 centimeters)

1 piece of print fabric, 12 by 18 inches

white glue

stapler

string or thin metallic trim

old magazines and catalogs

yellow yarn

HERE IS WHAT YOU DO:

1 Cut a piece of fabric to exactly cover one of the pieces of brown paper. Glue the fabric over the paper.

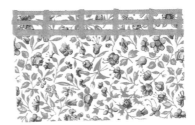

2 Cut the sides and bottom of the berry basket apart so that you have five pieces. Staple the pieces across the top of the fabric-covered paper lengthwise. This will be the roof frame of your sukkah.

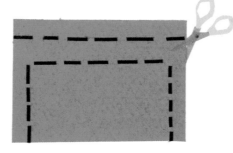

3 Trim 2 inches (5 centimeters) off the length of the second piece of paper. Cut a rectangle out of the paper so that you are left with a three-sided frame to form the opening for your shelter. Glue the frame to the front of the fabric-covered paper.

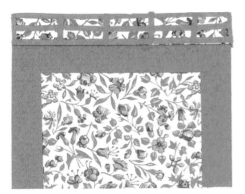

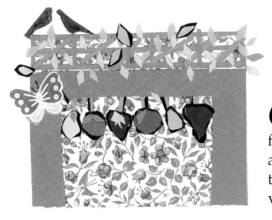

4 Weave pieces of green pipe cleaner to the roof frame for branches. Cut pictures of leaves and other greenery from old magazines and glue them among the pipe cleaner branches. You may want to cut out some birds and butterflies to glue on, too.

5 Cut 2-inch (5-centimeter) pieces of string and glue them so they hang down from the roof of the shelter with their ends tucked behind the paper frame. Cut pictures of fruits and vegetables to glue on the end of each string.

6 Glue green construction paper to the bottom of the picture to look like a grassy floor. Cut tables and chairs from old catalogs and glue them in place. You might also want to cut out things to put on the table, such as a vase of flowers, dishes, and candles.

7 Cut a 24-inch (60-centimeter) piece of yarn and staple one end to each side of the top of the picture to make a hanger.

What else can you cut out to add to your sukkah collage? Perhaps cut-up photos of family and friends could add people to your collage.

These grapes to hang from your sukkah are guaranteed to stay fresh!

SUKKAH GRAPES

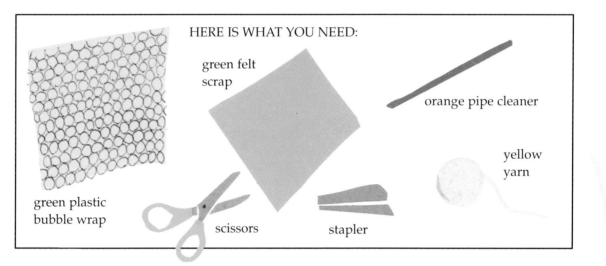

HERE IS WHAT YOU NEED:

green felt scrap

orange pipe cleaner

yellow yarn

green plastic bubble wrap

scissors

stapler

HERE IS WHAT YOU DO:

1 Cut a bunch of grapes out of the bubble wrap. You can do this by cutting around the bubbles so that there is one bubble grape at the bottom, two above it, then three, then four, then five, then six, then back to five again.

2 Cut a 6-inch (15-centimeter) piece of orange pipe cleaner. Fold it in half and twist it around itself to make the stem of the grapes. Staple the stem to the top of the grapes.

3 Cut a leaf from green felt. Staple the leaf next to the stem.

4 Cut an 18-inch (45-centimeter) piece of yarn for a hanger. Thread it through the twisted pipe cleaner and tie the two ends together.

Make one or more bunches of grapes to hang in your sukkah. If you do not have green bubble wrap, you can use clear bubble wrap. Ask an adult to cut a slit in the back of each bubble. To make green or purple grapes, just stuff each bubble with a piece of crumpled tissue paper in the color you want your grapes to be.

42

Make this little nest to tuck in the branches of your sukkah.

TWINE BIRD'S NEST

HERE IS WHAT YOU NEED:

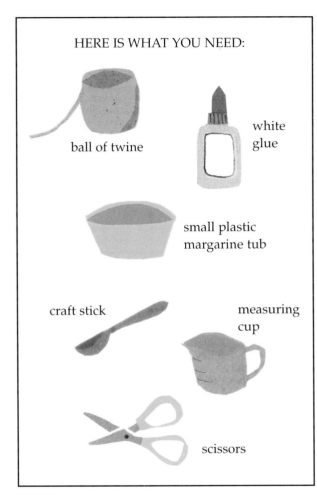

ball of twine

white glue

small plastic margarine tub

craft stick

measuring cup

scissors

HERE IS WHAT YOU DO:

1 Cut about one cupful of 1-inch (2.5-centimeter) pieces of twine.

2 Pour about ¼ cup of glue into the margarine tub. Add a few drops of water to thin the glue slightly. Mix the glue and water using the craft stick.

3 Add the cut twine pieces and mix them in the glue until they are thoroughly coated. All the glue should be absorbed. If it is not, add a few more pieces of twine.

4 Press the gluey twine into the bottom and sides of the tub to shape a nest. Let the nest dry completely before taking it out of the plastic tub.

Before you tuck your nest into the branches of your sukkah, you might want to add some eggs shaped from play dough, or an artificial bird.

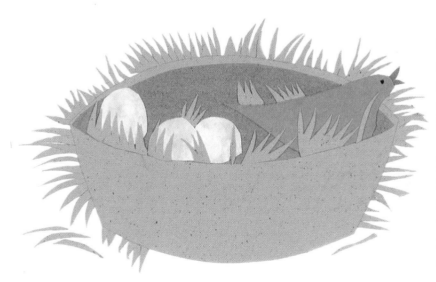

This vine picture holder will give you a place to display pictures of visitors to your sukkah, both past and present.

VINE PICTURE HOLDER

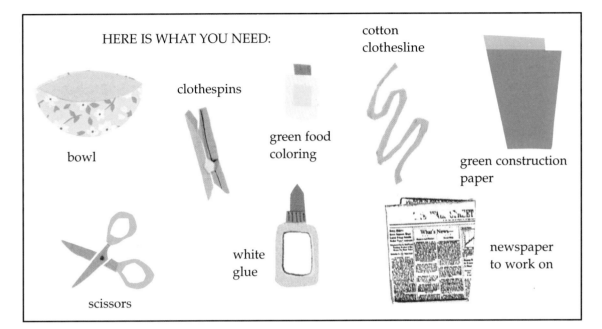

HERE IS WHAT YOU NEED:

cotton clothesline

clothespins

green food coloring

green construction paper

bowl

white glue

newspaper to work on

scissors

HERE IS WHAT YOU DO:

1 Cut a piece of clothesline long enough to string all the way across your sukkah.

2 Put enough water in the bowl to cover the clothesline. Add 8 drops of green food coloring to the water. Put the clothesline in the bowl for a few minutes to absorb the color. Take out the clothesline and carefully squeeze out the excess water before setting it on newspaper to dry. The rope will not be evenly colored, but will have a mottled green look.

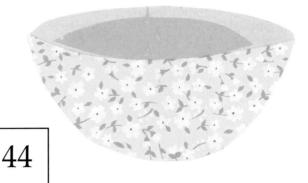

3 You will need a clothespin for each photograph you want to hang from the line. Cut a leaf from green construction paper to glue on the flat side of each clothespin.

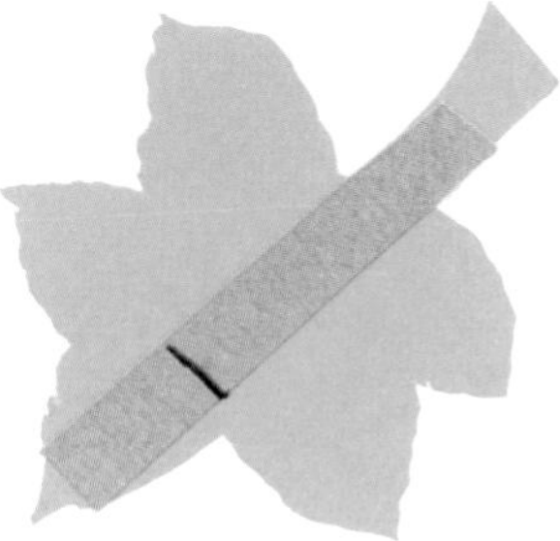

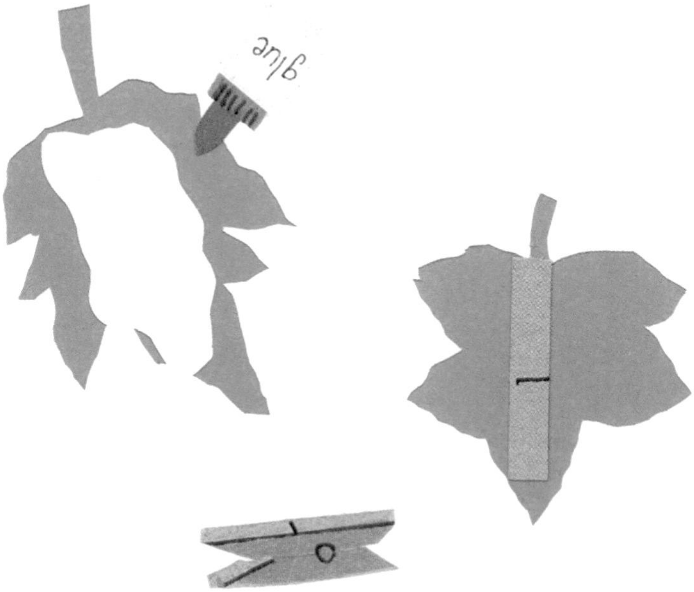

glue

4 Clip the clothespins along the clothesline vine and hang the vine across your sukkah.

Each year you can take new pictures and hang up the old pictures of people who have visited you in your sukkah. This is a wonderful way to collect years of sukkah memories.

45

The etrog looks like a very large, somewhat wrinkled lemon.

THE ETROG

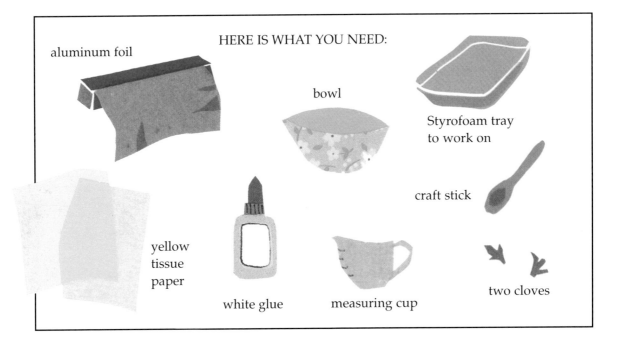

HERE IS WHAT YOU NEED:

aluminum foil

bowl

Styrofoam tray to work on

craft stick

yellow tissue paper

white glue

measuring cup

two cloves

HERE IS WHAT YOU DO:

1 Crumple up aluminum foil to make the shape of the etrog. Keep adding foil until it is the size of a real etrog, about 4 inches (10 centimeters) high and 3 inches (7.5 centimeters) wide at the bottom.

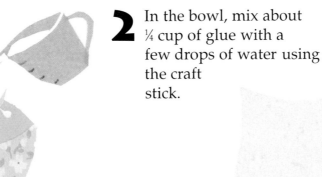

2 In the bowl, mix about ¼ cup of glue with a few drops of water using the craft stick.

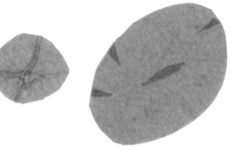

3 Cut a 12-inch (30-centimeter) square of yellow tissue paper.

4 Dip the tissue in the glue, then, starting from the bottom, wrap it up and around the foil etrog. Make sure the entire fruit is covered with yellow tissue paper. If a part is not covered, use a second sheet of tissue.

5 Break the head off a clove and glue it at the bottom of the fruit. Glue a whole clove, with the head down and the stick pointing up for a stem, at the top of the fruit.

6 Let this project dry completely on a Styrofoam tray.

These are the three kinds of branches required to make a lulav.

PALM, WILLOW, AND MYRTLE BRANCHES

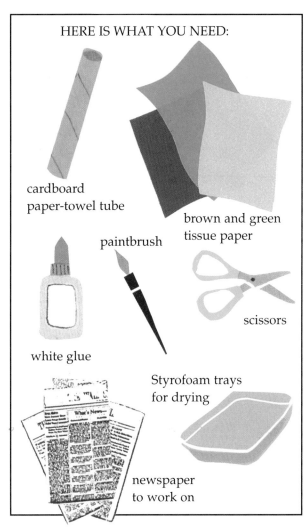

HERE IS WHAT YOU NEED:

cardboard
paper-towel tube

brown and green
tissue paper

paintbrush

scissors

white glue

Styrofoam trays
for drying

newspaper
to work on

HERE IS WHAT YOU DO:

1 Cut six strips from the tube that are as tall as the tube and about ¾ inch (2 centimeters) wide. Cut a point at the end of one of the strips for the palm branch.

2 Paint each strip with white glue and cover it with brown tissue paper.

3 Cut long willow leaves from green tissue paper and glue them along two of the branches, leaving the bottom 2 inches (5 centimeters) of the branch bare.

4 Cut tiny myrtle leaves from the green tissue paper and glue them along three of the branches, again leaving the bottom 2 inches of the branch bare.

Let the branches dry completely on Styrofoam trays before shaking them.

A special blessing is said while waving the lulav along with the etrog, up and down, north and south, east and west.

LULAV HOLDER

HERE IS WHAT YOU DO:

1 Cut all the way up one side of two of the tubes.

2 Roll the two tubes as tight as you can and slip them, side by side, into the third tube. The holder will now have two sections inside.

3 Use the paintbrush to cover the outside of the holder with glue. Start at one end of the holder and wrap the entire outside of the tube in twine.

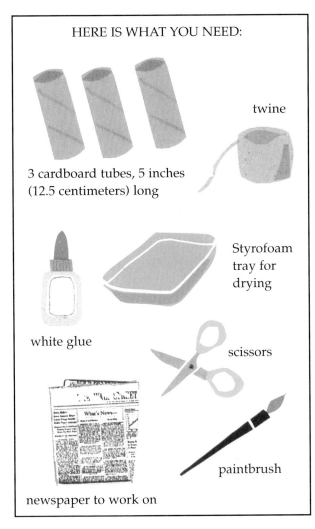

HERE IS WHAT YOU NEED:

twine

3 cardboard tubes, 5 inches (12.5 centimeters) long

white glue

Styrofoam tray for drying

scissors

paintbrush

newspaper to work on

4 Cut a piece of twine, 12 inches (30 centimeters) long. Glue the middle of the twine piece to the center of one side of the holder. Let the project dry completely on the Styrofoam tray.

To use the holder, put the two willow branches in one side of the holder and the three myrtle branches in the other side of the holder. Tie the palm branch to the front of the holder. Hold the etrog in your left hand and the lulav in your right hand. Hold the two together as you say a blessing over them in your sukkah or at your synagogue.

49

Make some fruit and vegetable hammocks to hang produce from the roof of your sukkah.

FRUIT AND VEGETABLE HAMMOCK

HERE IS WHAT YOU NEED:

small net bags that onions come in

yarn or string

scissors

HERE IS WHAT YOU DO:

1 Cut the bag so that you have a piece that is closed at the bottom and about 6 inches (15 centimeters) high. This will be the "hammock" holder for the fruit or vegetable.

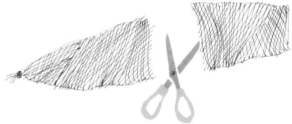

2 Cut two pieces of string or yarn, 24 inches (60 centimeters) long. Weave one piece in and out across one side of the top of the bag. Weave the other piece across the other side.

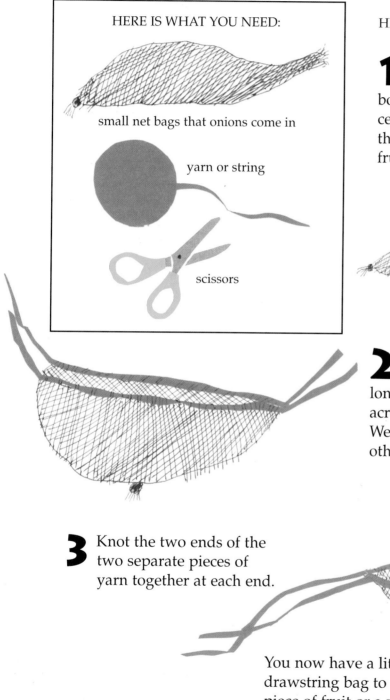

3 Knot the two ends of the two separate pieces of yarn together at each end.

You now have a little drawstring bag to hold a piece of fruit or a vegetable to hang in your sukkah.

SIMCHAT TORAH

The holiday following the last day of Sukkot is Simchat Torah. It celebrates the reading of the final portion of the Torah scroll.

After the last chapter of Deuteronomy, the final book of the Five Books of Moses contained in the Torah scrolls, is read, the scroll is at an end. There is a joyous celebration in the synagogue. Children dance and sing and carry flags. Adults carry the scrolls and march in a parade around the synagogue. And then the scrolls are rerolled and the readings begin again with the creation story in the first chapter of Genesis.

Wave your flag with pride in the Torah parade!

FLAG FOR SIMCHAT TORAH

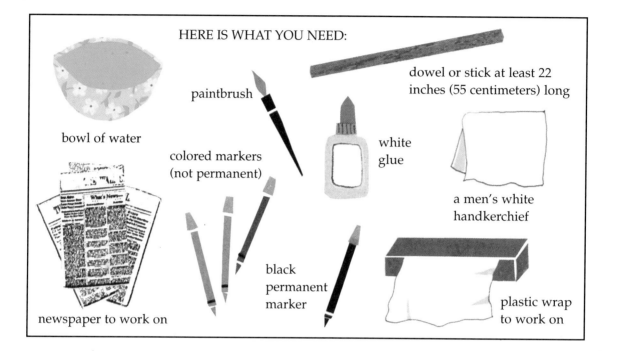

HERE IS WHAT YOU NEED:

paintbrush

dowel or stick at least 22 inches (55 centimeters) long

bowl of water

colored markers (not permanent)

white glue

a men's white handkerchief

newspaper to work on

black permanent marker

plastic wrap to work on

HERE IS WHAT YOU DO:

1 Working on newspaper, use the colored markers to color patches all over the handkerchief until it is completely covered. Do not use the black or brown markers for this part of the project because they tend to run into the other colors and cover them.

2 Place plastic wrap under the colored handkerchief. Paint over the colors with water to brighten them and run them together. Do this carefully using only enough water to dampen the fabric. Let the handkerchief dry.

3 Use the black permanent marker to draw the outline of a symbol of the season on the colored fabric. You could draw two stone tablets or the Torah. You decide what you would like on your flag.

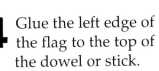

4 Glue the left edge of the flag to the top of the dowel or stick.

This little pin is perfect to wear on Simchat Torah.

TORAH PIN

HERE IS WHAT YOU NEED:

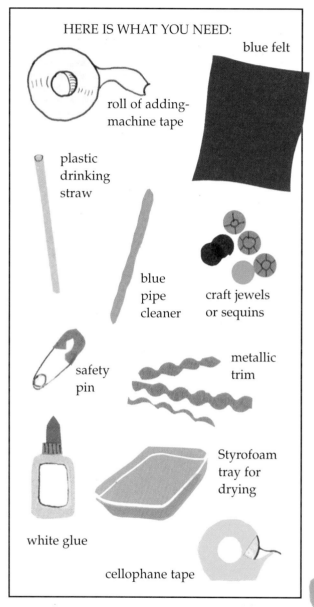

blue felt

roll of adding-machine tape

plastic drinking straw

blue pipe cleaner

craft jewels or sequins

safety pin

metallic trim

white glue

Styrofoam tray for drying

cellophane tape

HERE IS WHAT YOU DO:

1 Cut two 2-inch (5-centimeter) pieces from the straw. Cut a strip of adding tape, 12 inches (30 centimeters) long. If the tape is wider than the 2-inch straw pieces, trim the tape so that it is the same width as the straw pieces.

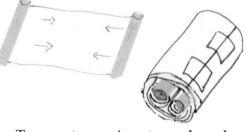

2 Tape a straw piece to each end of the paper strip. Roll the paper around the two straw pieces toward the center of the paper. Tape the rolled paper to hold it in place.

3 Cut two pieces of the pipe cleaner, 3 inches (7.5 centimeters) long. Slide one piece through each straw. Bend each end of the two pipe cleaners to make the handles.

4 Cut a piece of blue felt long enough to cover the paper but not the handles of the Torah. Cut it wide enough to wrap all the way around the paper rolls and overlap. Fringe the bottom of the felt. Glue the felt in place around the paper rolls.

5 Decorate the felt with metallic trim and little jewels or sequins.

Use a large safety pin to attach your Torah pin to your shirt.

HANUKKAH

Hanukkah is an eight-day celebration particularly beloved by children. It falls on the twenty-fifth of Kislev in the Jewish calendar, in late November or in December in the secular calendar.

The holiday commemorates a time when a small band of heroic Jews, led by Judah Maccabee, battled against the Syrian Greeks for religious freedom. The Jews won and recaptured Israel in 165 B.C.E.

Each night families light one additional candle on an eight-branched menorah. Children receive gifts and play with a top called a dreidel. Traditional foods include latkes, which are fried potato pancakes, usually served with applesauce.

The eight nights of the Hanukkah celebration are marked by lighting one additional candle on the menorah each evening.

MENORAH DECORATION

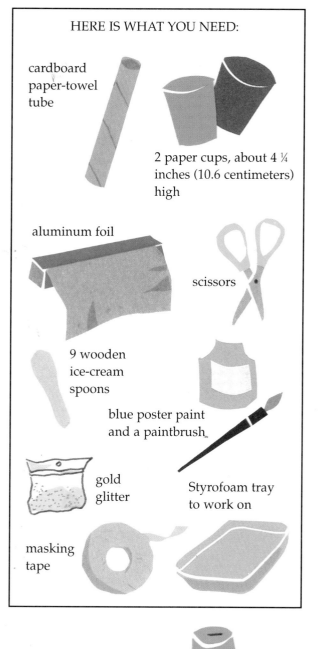

HERE IS WHAT YOU NEED:

cardboard paper-towel tube

2 paper cups, about 4 ¼ inches (10.6 centimeters) high

aluminum foil

scissors

9 wooden ice-cream spoons

blue poster paint and a paintbrush

gold glitter

Styrofoam tray to work on

masking tape

HERE IS WHAT YOU DO:

1 Cut off the top part of one cup so that you are left with a bottom piece about 1 ½ inches (3.8 centimeters) tall. Tape the bottom piece, bottom side up, to the center of the cardboard tube.

2 Turn the second cup upside down and tape the cardboard tube to the bottom of it so that the first cup piece is directly above the second cup. This will form the holder for the candles.

3 Cut eight evenly spaced ½-inch (1.3-centimeter) slits along the tube, four on each side of the cup at the center of the tube. The slits should be just big enough to slip the handle end of an ice-cream spoon in. Cut one slit in the center of the cup to hold the shamash, the helper candle used to light the other candles. You may need to ask an adult to do this for you.

4 Cover the entire project with aluminum foil. Run your finger along the foil to find the slits that you cut in the cup and the tube. Cut through the foil over the slits.

5 Paint the handle end of the nine ice-cream spoons blue. Let the spoons dry on the Styrofoam tray.

6 Paint the wide part of the nine spoons with glue and sprinkle them with gold glitter to look like flames.

7 Slip the wooden spoon candles into the slits in the holder.

A windowsill is a good place to display your menorah.

Make this oversized dreidel to play with this Hanukkah season.

BIG DREIDEL

HERE IS WHAT YOU NEED:

2 square tissue boxes

cardboard paper-towel tube

masking tape

blue permanent marker

blue yarn

scissors

clothespins

white glue

HERE IS WHAT YOU DO:

1 Cut the square out of the top of one tissue box. Cut from the top of the box down to the bottom of the box at each of the four corners.

2 Fold in the two corners of each of the four flaps. Rub glue all over the folded triangle-shaped flaps and push the glued flaps in toward the center of the box to form a point. Hold the box flaps in position with clothespins until the glue dries.

3 Cut the top square out of the second box. Rub glue around the inside of the box and slide the flat end of the first box inside the second box with the point sticking out at the bottom to form the dreidel. Let the glue dry before continuing.

4 Cut all the way down one side of the cardboard tube. Wrap it around itself to form a tube that is 1 inch (2.5 centimeters) across. Use masking tape to hold the handle in this position.

5 Cut a hole 1 inch across in the top of the dreidel. Rub glue on the bottom half of the tube and slip it into the hole as far as it will go.

6 Cover the dreidel base with aluminum foil.

7 Coat the handle with glue and wrap it with blue yarn to completely cover it.

8 Put a band of masking tape around the base of the dreidel. Coat the tape with glue, then wrap blue yarn around the base until the tape is completely covered.

9 Use the blue marker to draw one of the four Hebrew letters in the following order, from right to left, on each of the four sides of the dreidel.

נ ג ה ש

59

Make this gift bag to hold a Hanukkah surprise for someone on your gift list.

DREIDEL GIFT BAG

HERE IS WHAT YOU NEED:

plastic gallon milk jug for drying bag on

paintbrush

blue poster paint

paper shopping bag with attached handles, any size

thin metallic trim

white glue

stapler

newspaper to work on

scissors

HERE IS WHAT YOU DO:

1 Cut the bottom half of the bag into a point to make a dreidel shape. Staple the sides of the cut point shut.

2 Paint the outside of the bag blue. Slip the bag over the plastic jug to allow it to dry smoothly on all sides.

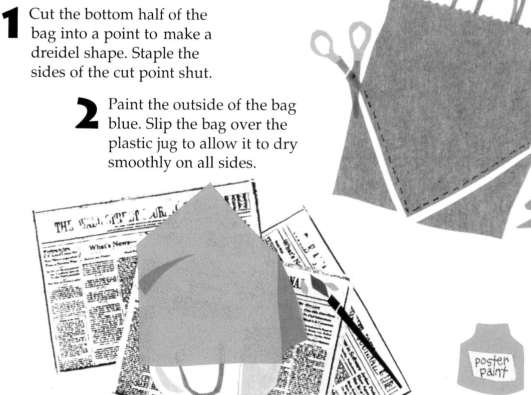

poster paint

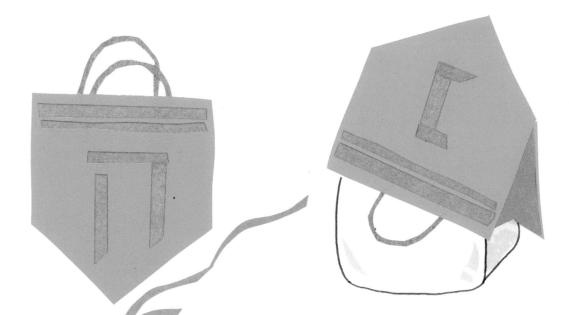

3 Glue two rows of metallic trim at the top of both sides of the bag. Shape two of the Hebrew letters found on a dreidel (see page 59) from the metallic trim. Glue one letter on each side of the bag. Slip the bag over the plastic jug again to dry.

Wrap a surprise in tissue paper and tuck it in this pretty gift bag.

*This Star of David would make a nice
Hanukkah gift for someone on your list.*

WINDOW STAR OF DAVID

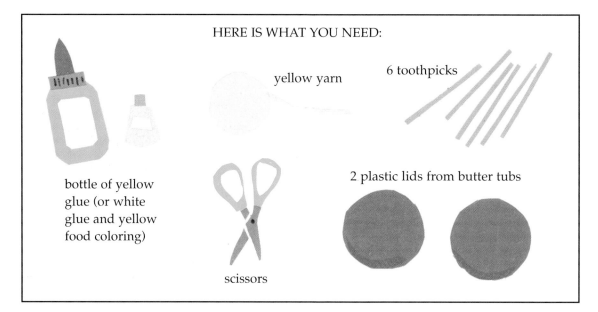

HERE IS WHAT YOU NEED:

yellow yarn

6 toothpicks

bottle of yellow
glue (or white
glue and yellow
food coloring)

2 plastic lids from butter tubs

scissors

HERE IS WHAT YOU DO:

1 If you do not have colored glue,
make your own by mixing four
drops of yellow food coloring in
about ¼ cup of glue.

2 Cover three toothpicks by dipping
them in yellow glue and shape
them into a triangle on the plastic lid.
Fill the triangle with yellow glue and
place the lid and triangle on a flat surface to dry completely. Do the same
thing on the other lid with the other
three toothpicks.

3 When both triangles are dry,
peel them off the plastic lids.
Glue them together in the shape
of a Star of David.

4 Glue a yarn hanger on
the back of the star.

If any of the points on the star seem too
sharp, trim them off with scissors before
hanging your decoration in a sunny window.

TU B'SHEVAT

Tu B'Shevat is the fifteenth of Shevat in the
Jewish calendar—the first day of spring in Israel.
It falls well before springtime in North America—
in late January or in February.

The celebration is also known as the birthday of
the trees. Some Jews celebrate by planting trees or
seeds. Others celebrate the holiday by purchasing trees
to be planted in Israel. Many people participate in a
Tu B'Shevat seder where they eat foods that could
be grown in Israel: fruits such as dates and figs,
and nuts such as almonds.

Several of these reminders of the birthday of trees would make charming table decorations for a Tu B'Shevat seder.

STICK TREE

HERE IS WHAT YOU NEED:

brown yarn

modeling clay

a branch about 12 inches (30 centimeters) long

white glue

scissors

piece of burlap

green tissue paper

HERE IS WHAT YOU DO:

1 Roll a ball of clay about 2 inches (5 centimeters) across. Press lightly on the ball to flatten the bottom.

2 Cut lots of ½-inch (1.3-centimeter) squares of tissue paper and crumple each square. Glue the crumpled squares all over one end of the stick to look like leaves on a tree.

3 Plant the other end of the stick in the ball of clay.

4 Cut an 8-inch (20-centimeter) square of burlap. Tie the burlap around the clay ball at the base of the tree to look like a tree with a root ball all ready to be planted.

Plant this little pot with parsley seeds on Tu B'Shevat and you will have parsley in time for Passover.

PARSLEY TREES PLANTER

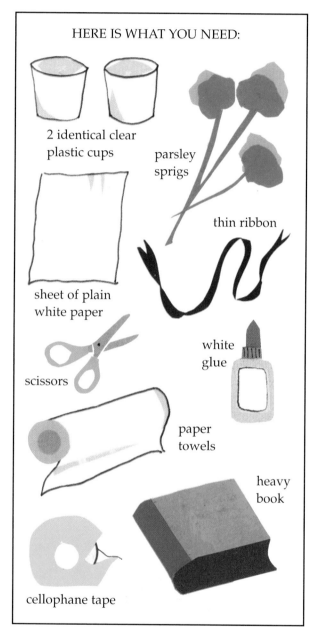

HERE IS WHAT YOU NEED:

2 identical clear plastic cups

parsley sprigs

thin ribbon

sheet of plain white paper

scissors

white glue

paper towels

heavy book

cellophane tape

HERE IS WHAT YOU DO:

1 Wrap the piece of white paper around the outside of one of the cups and hold it in place with a small piece of tape. Trim away excess paper above and below the cup. Carefully remove the tape and neatly cut away all but about 1 inch (2.5 centimeters) of the overlap of paper along the side of the cup. You should now have a piece of paper that fits neatly inside one of the cups. If it still does not quite fit, trim away any excess paper so that it does.

2 Put the paper liner down flat on a table and glue 3 or 4 little parsley "trees" onto the paper. Trim the stems of the parsley, if necessary, so that the parsley is not taller than the cup. Make sure your design will be right side up when you put it back into the cup.

3 Put the paper inside the cup. Put the other cup inside the first cup so that the paper is between the two cups. Be careful to keep the parsley "trees" in place.

4 Tie a pretty ribbon around the space at the top of the two cups.

Put a few stones and some potting soil in the planter and plant some parsley seeds. Don't forget to keep your planter in a sunny window and water it every day or two.

When people donate trees to be planted in Israel, they are usually given a certificate. This frame makes an extra special holder for a tree certificate.

TREE CERTIFICATE FRAME

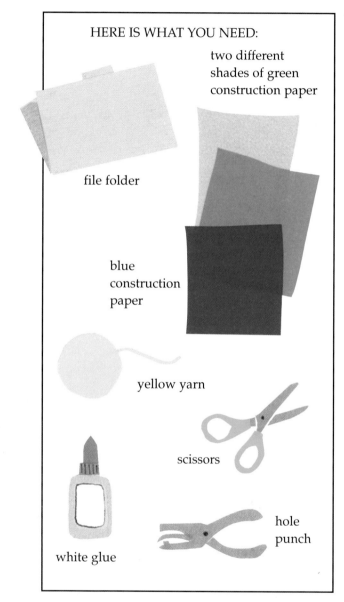

HERE IS WHAT YOU NEED:

two different shades of green construction paper

file folder

blue construction paper

yellow yarn

scissors

white glue

hole punch

HERE IS WHAT YOU DO:

1 Cut the tab off the file folder. Cut a rectangle out of the front of the folder so that you are left with a 1 ½-inch (3.8-centimeter) rim around the entire front of the folder.

2 Open the folder and glue a piece of blue paper on the inside back of the folder to cover it.

3 The frame will hang so that it is taller than it is wide, with the opening on the right side. Punch two holes in the top inside of the folder. String a 12-inch (30-centimeter) piece of yarn through the two holes and tie the ends together to make a hanger.

4 Put glue along the top and bottom inside of the folder and close it to glue the front frame to the back of the folder.

5 Cut leaf shapes from the green papers. Glue them around the frame of the folder to cover it.

The side of this frame has been left open so that you can easily slip a tree certificate into it.

69

Make a tzedakah box just for Tu B'Shevat.

TREE TZEDAKAH BOX

HERE IS WHAT YOU NEED:

black marker

brown and green construction paper

brown poster paint

paintbrush

cellophane tape

cardboard paper-towel tube

small plastic cap from detergent or fabric softener

two shades of green tissue paper

coin

alphabet macaroni

white glue

masking tape

newspaper to work on

HERE IS WHAT YOU DO:

1 Cut off one end of the tube so that the tube is 8 inches (20 centimeters) long. About 1 inch (2.5 centimeters) down from the top, cut a squirrel hole in the tube about 2 by 1 inches (5 by 2.5 centimeters).

2 Paint the tube brown and let it dry completely.

3 First check the fit of your plastic cap (see step 7). Then tape a piece of green paper around the plastic cap to cover it. Glue the macaroni letters to spell Tu B'Shevat around the side of the cap. You can break off a little piece of macaroni to make the apostrophe between the "B" and the "S."

TU B' SHEVAT

glue

4 Cut a 10-inch (25-centimeter) square from each of two different shades of green tissue paper. Set one square on top of the other. Rub glue around the top inside of the tube. Pick the two squares of tissue up at the center and tuck the center portion of the tissue squares into the top of the tube tree. The tissue should stick out of the top of the tube to resemble leaves.

5 On brown paper, draw a squirrel head small enough to fit in the hole in the tree. Draw two squirrel paws. Cut out the head and paws.

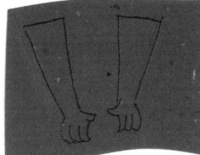

6 Put masking tape on one side of the coin. Apply glue to the masking tape side of the coin and attach the coin to the tube, below the hole. Glue the squirrel paws over the top of the coin with the ends tucked in the hole. Glue the squirrel head behind the paws, peeking out of the hole. The squirrel should look like it is holding the coin.

7 Slide the cardboard tube into the plastic cap. It should fit snuggly over the inner liner of the cap.

Drop your tzedakah coins in the hole in the tree. To get them out, just lift the tree off the base and empty the plastic cap.

PURIM

Purim, the 14th of Adar in the Jewish calendar, occurs
in late February or early March in the secular calendar.
The holiday begins with the reading of the megillah, the story
of Queen Esther, wife of the Persian king Ahasuerus who ruled
in the 5th century B.C.E. Haman, the prime minister, was plotting
to kill the Persian Jews. Esther used her influence with the king
to save the Jews. Haman was hanged for his evil plot.

It is the custom to wear costumes to a Purim festival.
Children like to dress up as Queen Esther, King Ahasuerus,
Esther's uncle Mordecai, or the evil Haman with his
three-cornered hat. When the story is read, children use
noisemakers called groggers to drown out the
sound of the evil Haman's name.

Cookielike pastries called *hamantaschen* are served on Purim.
They are triangle-shaped to look like Haman's hat.

*Tell the story of Purim with
these four finger puppets.*

PURIM PUPPETS

HERE IS WHAT YOU DO:

1 Stuff a cotton ball into the tip of four fingers of the glove. Tie a piece of yarn under each cotton ball to hold it in place to form a head.

2 Cut a 1-inch (2.5-centimeter) circle of pink felt for Queen Esther. Glue the circle on the pinky finger of the glove. Cut a crown from yellow felt and glue it on her head. Decorate the crown with metallic trim. Draw on a face with the markers. Glue pieces of brown yarn on each side of the head for hair.

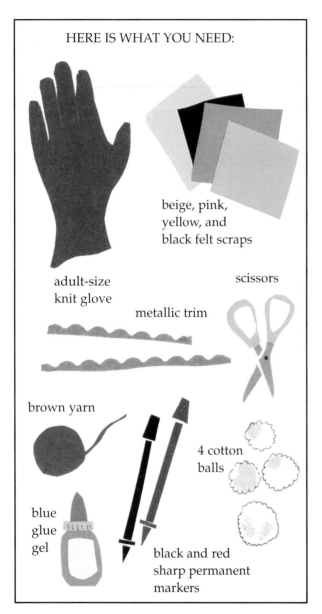

HERE IS WHAT YOU NEED:

beige, pink, yellow, and black felt scraps

adult-size knit glove

scissors

metallic trim

brown yarn

4 cotton balls

blue glue gel

black and red sharp permanent markers

3 To make King Ahasuerus, cut a 1-inch circle from beige felt and glue it on the next finger for the face. Cut a crown from yellow felt and decorate it with metallic trim. Glue the crown to the top of the head. Draw a face with markers, and glue on hair and a beard cut from brown yarn.

4 To make Mordecai, cut a 1-inch circle from the beige felt and glue it to the next finger. Draw a face with markers. Glue on brown yarn hair and beard.

5 To make the evil Haman, cut a 1-inch circle from beige felt and glue it on the last finger. Cut a triangle hat from black felt and glue it to the top of the head. Draw a face with markers. Cut hair and a small beard from brown yarn and glue it in place.

Slip your hand into the glove puppet and tell the story of how Queen Esther saved her people.

*Make a king or queen crown
to wear to your Purim celebration.*

PURIM CROWNS

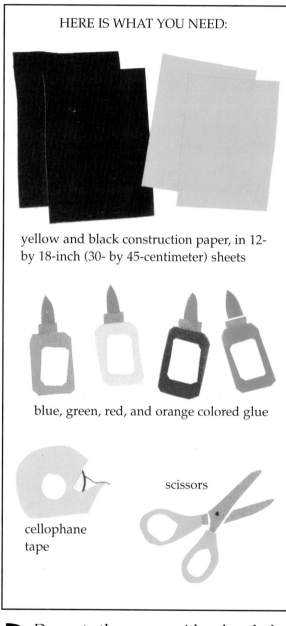

HERE IS WHAT YOU NEED:

yellow and black construction paper, in 12-
by 18-inch (30- by 45-centimeter) sheets

blue, green, red, and orange colored glue

cellophane
tape

scissors

HERE IS WHAT YOU DO
TO MAKE EACH CROWN:

1 Cut a sheet of yellow construction paper in half lengthwise
so you have two 6- by 18-inch (15-
by 45-centimeter) strips. Tape the
two strips together, end to end.
Measure the strip around your
head and cut the strip to fit with
enough paper left over to overlap
the ends for taping.

2 Cut a pointed crown across
the top of the paper. You can
make the crown as tall or as
short as you wish.

3 Decorate the crown with colored glue
and let it dry. Then tape it into a circle
to fit your head.

TO MAKE ESTHER'S CROWN:

1 Fold a sheet of black construction paper in half crosswise so that it measures 12 by 9 inches (30 by 22.5 centimeters). Starting at the fold, cut an 8- by 8-inch (20- by 20-centimeter) piece, cutting in wavy lines to look like hair.

2 Open the wavy hair and tape the top inside the back and sides of the crown. If the hair is so long that it stops the crown from sitting snugly on your head, trim the hair along the bottom until the crown fits.

TO MAKE AHASUERUS'S CROWN:

1 Fold a sheet of black construction paper in half crosswise so that it measures 12 by 9 inches. Cutting in a wavy line to make a beard, trim the folded paper all around so that it is about 8 by 11 inches (20 by 27.5 centimeters). Starting on the fold, cut a 3- by 5-inch (7.5- by 12.5-centimeter) rounded-corner rectangle out of the side of the paper.

2 Open up the paper and tape it to the front and sides of the crown so that the opening for the face is at the top and the paper beard is below.

Find a friend to be your king or queen and make these two Purim festival crowns together.

*Give Haman a good shaking
this Purim—he deserves it!*

HAMAN SHAKER

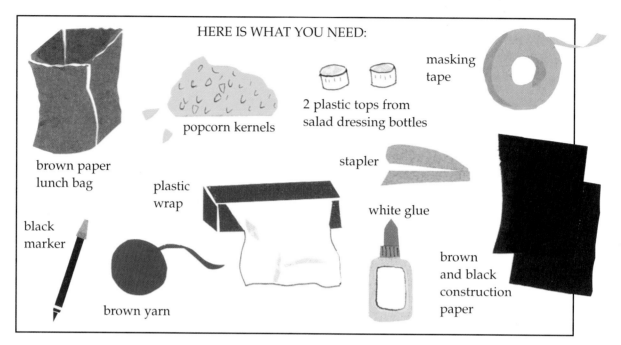

HERE IS WHAT YOU NEED:

masking tape

2 plastic tops from
salad dressing bottles

popcorn kernels

brown paper
lunch bag

stapler

plastic
wrap

white glue

black
marker

brown
and black
construction
paper

brown yarn

HERE IS WHAT YOU DO:

1 From black paper, cut a triangle
with 7-inch (17.5-centimeter) sides.
Fold each side up and staple the
fold to make Haman's hat.

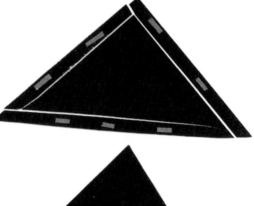

2 Put a handful of popcorn
kernels in the lunch bag. Fold
the top of the bag over three times
and staple the fold to hold it. Staple
the hat to the top front of the bag.

3 Cut two ½-inch (1.3-centimeter) circles from brown construction paper for eyeballs. Put one in each plastic bottle top. Cover each top with plastic wrap and tape the ends behind the eyes (the top of the plastic tops). The paper eyes should move about freely under the plastic wrap. Glue both eyes to the bag below the hat.

4 Draw on a nose and mouth with the black marker.

5 Cut brown yarn to make hair and a beard and glue them in place.

Surprise one of your friends with this royal treat!

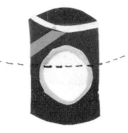

CROWN TREAT BASKET

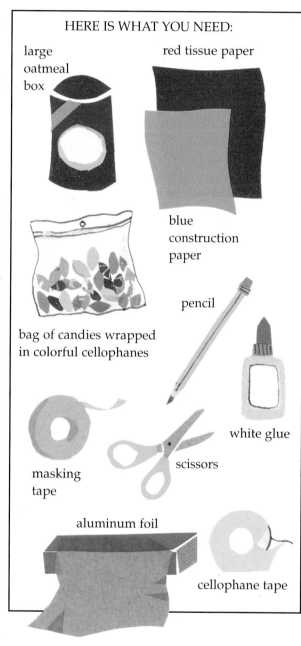

HERE IS WHAT YOU NEED:

large oatmeal box

red tissue paper

blue construction paper

bag of candies wrapped in colorful cellophanes

pencil

white glue

masking tape

scissors

aluminum foil

cellophane tape

HERE IS WHAT YOU DO:

1 Cut off the top portion of the oatmeal box so that the box is about 5 inches (12.5 centimeters) tall. Cut points around the cut edge of the box bottom to make it look like a crown.

2 Cover the box crown, inside and outside, with aluminum foil.

3 Trace around the bottom of the crown on the blue paper. Cut out the circle.

4 Cover the bottom of the box with strips of masking tape formed into a ring, sticky side out. Glue the blue circle to the tape on the bottom of the box.

5 Tape some of the candies around the crown to look like jewels.

6 Tuck a 12-inch (30-centimeter) square of red tissue paper inside the crown and fill the crown with the rest of the candies.

PASSOVER

Passover, the second of the three major pilgrimage festivals, is a seven- or eight-day springtime holiday commemorating Moses leading the Jewish people out of slavery in Egypt. Also called Pesach, Passover is the fifteenth of Nissan in the Jewish calendar, which is usually some time in April in the secular one.

On the first and second evening of Passover, families gather for a ritual dinner called a *seder*. During the meal, they read from a Haggadah — a book telling the story of the Jewish people's exodus from Egypt. Matzoh, unleavened bread, is eaten for eight days as a reminder that the Israelites did not have time to allow their bread to rise as they fled from slavery in Egypt.

An extra setting is often left at the seder table for the prophet Elijah, who will one day come to announce the arrival of the Messiah.

Moses' mother hid him in the bulrushes to escape the Egyptian Pharaoh's decree to kill all firstborn Jewish male babies.

MOSES IN THE BULRUSHES

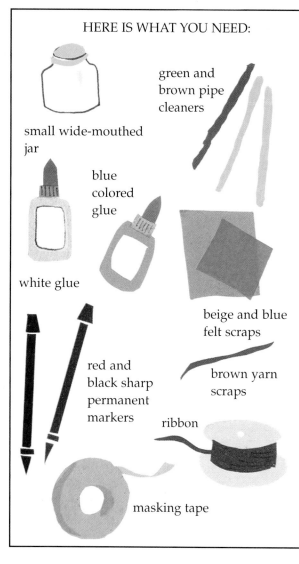

HERE IS WHAT YOU NEED:

small wide-mouthed jar

green and brown pipe cleaners

blue colored glue

white glue

beige and blue felt scraps

red and black sharp permanent markers

brown yarn scraps

ribbon

masking tape

1 Wrap a 12-inch (30-centimeter) pipe cleaner around itself to make a tiny basket about 1½ inches (3.8 centimeters) long. Trim off any extra pipe cleaner.

2 Cut a tiny circle from the beige felt to be the head of the baby Moses. Use the markers to draw a face on the felt circle. Glue on some bits of brown yarn for hair. Glue the head at one end of the basket.

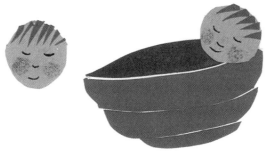

3 Cut a tiny blanket from the blue felt. Glue the blanket below the baby's head over the rest of the inside of the basket.

4 Squeeze about ¼ inch (0.6 centimeter) of blue glue over the inside bottom of the jar. Carefully set the baby in the basket inside the jar on the blue glue.

5 Cut six pieces of green pipe cleaner, each 2 inches (5 centimeters) long. Stand the pieces around the baby basket to look like bulrushes.

6 Cover the top and sides of the jar lid with masking tape. Cut a circle of blue felt to cover the top of the lid. Cover the sides and the top of the lid with white glue. Glue the blue felt circle to the top of the lid and glue ribbon around the side of the lid.

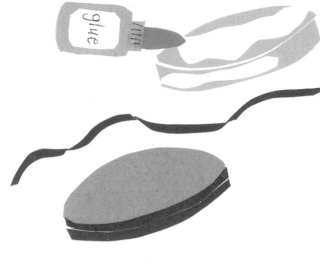

7 Let the blue glue "water" in the jar dry for several days before putting the top on the jar.

83

*Make this pretty spring centerpiece for your
Passover seder table. These spring blossoms will
last through many seasons instead of just a few days.*

FLOWER BRANCH CENTERPIECE

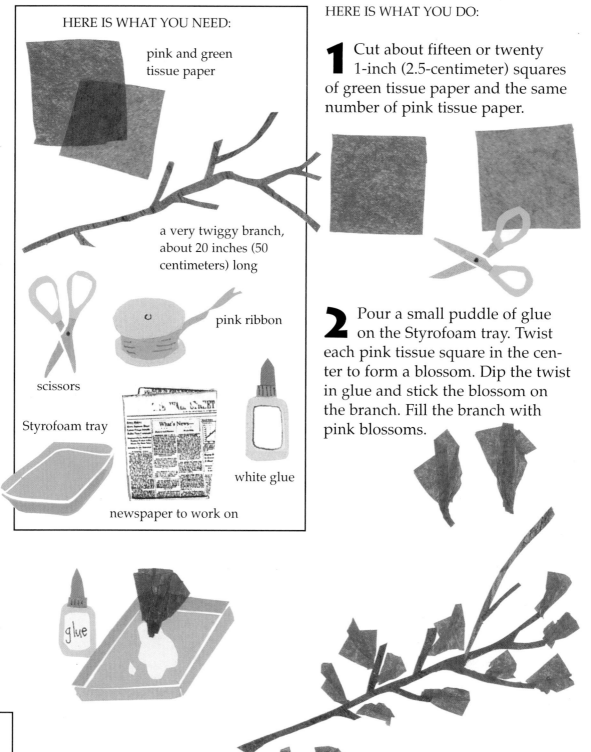

HERE IS WHAT YOU NEED:

pink and green tissue paper

a very twiggy branch, about 20 inches (50 centimeters) long

pink ribbon

scissors

Styrofoam tray

white glue

newspaper to work on

HERE IS WHAT YOU DO:

1 Cut about fifteen or twenty 1-inch (2.5-centimeter) squares of green tissue paper and the same number of pink tissue paper.

2 Pour a small puddle of glue on the Styrofoam tray. Twist each pink tissue square in the center to form a blossom. Dip the twist in glue and stick the blossom on the branch. Fill the branch with pink blossoms.

3 Twist each green tissue square in the center to form a leaf. Dip the center of each leaf in glue and stick a leaf next to each blossom.

4 Tie a pretty bow at the base of the branch.

85

The contents of these candleholders can be changed for use in different seasons of the Jewish year. You might want to put small objects in the jars, such as small dreidels for Hanukkah.

GLASS CANDLEHOLDERS

HERE IS WHAT YOU NEED:

2 small glass baby-food jars with lids

modeling clay

white glue

2 8-inch (20-centimeter) candles

scissors

masking tape

2 metal twist-off soda caps

pink nail polish

2 tiny bunches of small pink artificial flowers

HERE IS WHAT YOU DO:

1 Paint the edge of both jar lids and the sides of both bottle caps with pink nail polish.

2 Put a bunch of pink flowers, heads first, into each jar. You may need to cut off the stems to make them fit. Put the lid back on each jar and turn the jars over so that the lids are at the bottom and the flowers are right side up.

3 Put a square of masking tape on the flat top of each bottle cap and in the center of the glass top of each inverted jar. Glue the caps, tape to tape, to the tops of the jars to hold the candles. Let the glue dry.

4 Press a small amount of modeling clay into each cap, then stand a candle in the clay. Twist each candle around so that the clay packs around the edges of the caps to help hold the candles in place.

87

It is traditional for the leader of the seder to have a soft pillow to recline on.

T-SHIRT PILLOW

HERE IS WHAT YOU NEED:

adult-size T-shirt in yellow or another bright color

yellow felt and three other bright colors of felt

thin ribbon in two bright colors

two rubber bands

fabric glue

large bag of fiberfill

scissors

HERE IS WHAT YOU DO:

1 Gather the bottom of the T-shirt about 3 inches (7.5 centimeters) up from the bottom. Hold the gather closed with a rubber band.

2 Stuff the entire shirt with fiberfill.

3 Gather up the top of the shirt, including the sleeves, and close it with a rubber band.

4 From each color of ribbon, cut two pieces, each 18 inches (45 centimeters) long. Hold two different colors of ribbon together and tie a bow around the rubber bands at each end.

5 Cut a 4 ½-inch (11.3-centimeter) flower head from each of the three different colors of felt. Cut a yellow center for each flower.

6 Glue the three flowers to one side of the pillow to decorate it.

SHAVUOT

Shavuot is the third of the three major pilgrimage festivals.
It is a springtime holiday of first fruits that usually occurs in
May or early June—the sixth of Sivan in the Jewish calendar.

Shavuot, known as a time of milk and honey, celebrates
the day that Moses was given the Ten Commandments
by God on Mount Sinai. It is traditional to eat only
dairy foods during this celebration.

Moses receiving the Ten Commandments on Mount Sinai is a dramatic moment in Jewish history.

MOSES AND THE TEN COMMANDMENTS

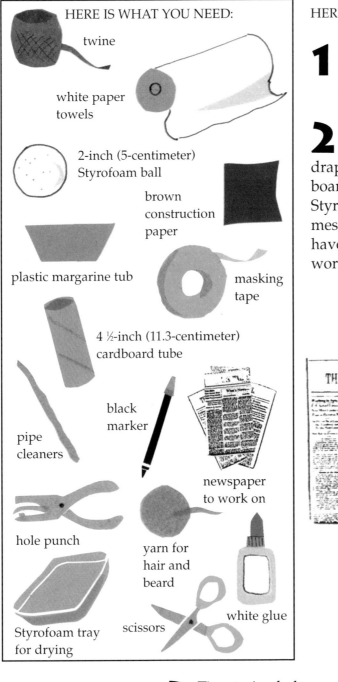

HERE IS WHAT YOU NEED:

twine

white paper towels

2-inch (5-centimeter) Styrofoam ball

brown construction paper

plastic margarine tub

masking tape

4 ½-inch (11.3-centimeter) cardboard tube

black marker

pipe cleaners

newspaper to work on

hole punch

yarn for hair and beard

white glue

Styrofoam tray for drying

scissors

HERE IS WHAT YOU DO:

1 In the plastic margarine tub, mix ¼ cup of water into a cup of white glue.

2 Dip a square of paper towel into the glue mixture and drape it over the top of the cardboard tube that is standing on the Styrofoam tray. (This is a very messy project, so make sure you have put newspaper over your work area.)

3 Tie a twine belt around the middle of the tube.

4 Glue the Styrofoam ball to the top of the tube for the head. Wrap pipe cleaner arms around the back of the tube to stick out the front on each side. Use masking tape to hold them in place at the back of the figure.

5 Dip another paper towel square in the glue and drape it over the top and back of the Styrofoam ball head. Tie a piece of twine around the top part of the head and headpiece.

6 Punch eyes from the brown paper and glue them to the head. Cut a yarn beard to glue to the front of the face.

7 Cut two tablets from the brown paper and use markers to write on them. Fold a pipe cleaner arm around each tablet and glue them in place. Let the project dry completely before removing it from the tray.

On Shavuot we welcome the first fruits of spring. Surprise someone special with this pretty little Shavuot basket.

SHAVUOT BASKET

HERE IS WHAT YOU NEED:

plastic cap from a large bottle of salad dressing

thin ribbon

green yarn

rickrack trim

fruit- and vegetable-shaped gummy candies

blue pipe cleaner

alphabet macaroni

white glue

masking tape

HERE IS WHAT YOU DO:

1 Cover the outside of the cap with masking tape. Glue on two rows of rickrack trim to decorate it.

2 Glue macaroni letters to spell Shavuot on the outside of the cap.

3 Squeeze glue all over the inside of the cap. Cut a 6-inch (15-centimeter) piece of blue pipe cleaner. Stick the two ends of the pipe cleaner in the glue in the cap to form a handle for the cap basket.

4 Cut up bits of green yarn. Put the yarn bits in the glue in the basket to look like grass.

5 Squeeze glue over the yarn grass. Put four different candy fruits and vegetables in the basket. Squeeze more glue over them to hold them in place.

6 Tie a piece of ribbon in a bow around the basket handle.

93

Paper cuttings are a traditional part of decorating for Shavuot.

HOOP-FRAMED PAPER CUTTING

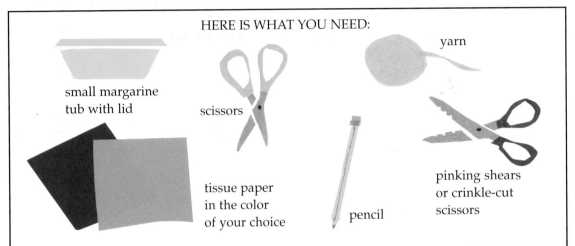

HERE IS WHAT YOU NEED:

small margarine tub with lid

scissors

tissue paper in the color of your choice

pencil

yarn

pinking shears or crinkle-cut scissors

HERE IS WHAT YOU DO:

1 Cut the rim off the top of the margarine tub. Cut the center out of the lid of the tub. This will give you a holder for your paper cutting that works like an embroidery hoop.

2 Cut a 4-inch (10-centimeter) piece of yarn and tie the two ends together around the rim of the container to make a hanger for the hoop.

3 Trace around the lid rim on tissue paper. Cut around the line with pinking shears about 1 inch (2.5 centimeters) out from the traced circle.